Fact Finders®

P9-EGK-229

PEOPLE YOU
SHOULD KNOW

STEPHEN HAWKING

Get to Know the Man Behind the Theory

by Cristina Oxtra

Consultant: Gayle Nelson Evans
Lecturer in Science Education
University of Florida, Gainesville

CAPSTONE PRESS
a capstone imprint

Fact Finders Books are published by Capstone Press
1710 Roe Crest Drive, North Mankato, Minnesota 56003
www.capstonepub.com

**Library of Congress Cataloging-in-Publication data is available
on the Library of Congress website.**
Names: Oxtra, Cristina, author.
Title: Stephen Hawking : get know the man behind the theory / by Cristina Oxtra.
Other titles: Fact finders. People you should know.
Description: North Mankato, Minnesota : Capstone Press, a Capstone imprint,
  [2020] | Series: Fact finders. People you should know. | Includes
  bibliographical references and index. | Audience: 8–9. | Audience: K to
  grade 3.
Identifiers: LCCN 2019005999| ISBN 9781543571868 (hardcover) | ISBN
  1543571867 (hardcover) | ISBN 9781543574685 (paperback) | ISBN 1543574688
  (paperback) | ISBN 9781543571936 (eBook PDF) | ISBN 154357193X (eBook PDF)
Subjects: LCSH: Hawking, Stephen, 1942-2018—Juvenile literature. |
  Physicists—Great Britain—Biography—Juvenile literature. | People with
  disabilities—Biography—Juvenile literature. | Cosmology—Juvenile
  literature.
Classification: LCC QC16.H33 O98 2020 | DDC 530.092 [B]—dc23
LC record available at https://lccn.loc.gov/2019005999

Editorial Credits
Mari Bolte, editor; Kayla Rossow, designer; Tracy Cummins, media researcher;
Tori Abraham, production specialist

Photo Credits
Alamy: Chung/Xinhua, 22; Getty Images: Jonathan Brady, 26, Staff/Mirrorpix, 19; Newscom: ABD RABBO/SIPA, Cover,
Andrew Parsons/ZUMA Press, 6, Balkis Press/ABACA, 24, Derek Storm/Everett Collection, 29, Steven Paston/ZUMA Press,
4; Science Source: Corbin O'Grady Studio, 21, HARALD RITSCH, 16; Shutterstock: Feng Cheng, 18, Pajor Pawel, 9, PoohFotoz,
10, REDPIXEL.PL, 13; The Image Works: Hedgecoe/TopFoto, 15

Source Notes
page 5, line 1: "Stephen Hawking Speaks at London 2012 Paralympic Games Opening Ceremony." https://www.paralympic.org/video/stephen-
hawking-speaks-london-2012-paralympic-games-opening-ceremony. Accessed 2 August 2018.
page 6, line 10: *Hawking.* Dir. Stephen Finnigan Film. 2013.
page 7, line 3: *Hawking.*
page 7, line 10: *Hawking.*
page 8, line 3: Stephen Hawking. *My Brief History.* New York: Bantam Books, 2013, p. 24
page 9, line 1: *Hawking.*
page 11, line 7: *Hawking.*
page 17, sidebar: Pallab Ghosh. "Hawking Says Trump's Climate Stance Could Damage Earth." https://www.bbc.com/news/science-environment-
40461726?ocid=socialflow_facebook&ns_mchannel=social&ns_campaign=bbcnews&ns_source=facebook. Accessed 16 August 2018.
page 25, line 1: Sean Alfano. "Stephen Hawking Wins Top Science Award." https://www.cbsnews.com/news/stephen-hawking-wins-top-science-
award/. Accessed 5 August 2018.
page 25, sidebar: Monica Tan. "Stephen Hawking Tells Fans Zayn Malik Could Still Be in a Parallel One Direction." https://www.theguardian.com/
culture/2015/apr/27/stephen-hawking-tells-fans-zayn-malik-could-still-be-in-a-parallel-one-direction. Accessed 9 August 2018.
page 26, line 7: UNESCO. Twitter Post. March 14, 2018, 3:48 AM. https://twitter.com/UNESCO/status/973873397489946624
page 27, line 7: David Ewing Duncan. "A Little Device That's Trying to Read Your Thoughts. "https://www.nytimes.com/2012/04/03/science/ibrain-a-
device-that-can-read-thoughts.html?mtrref=www.google.com&gwh=3634F6B4AEB2547445E22D8212CFFF85&gwt=pay. Accessed 23 August 2018.
page 29, line 7: Alok Jha. "Stephen Hawking Marks 70th Birthday with Speech to Leading Cosmologists." https://www.theguardian.com/
science/2012/jan/08/stephen-hawking-70-cambridge-speech. Accessed 13 August 2018.
page 29, line 9: "Stephen Hawking's Hope for Humanity." http://www.humanexcellence.org/a-message-from-stephen-hawking-it-can-be-done/.
Accessed 13 August 2018.

TABLE OF CONTENTS

BE BRAVE

Music, fireworks, and the cheers of 80,000 people brought London's Olympic Stadium to life. The 2012 World **Paralympic** Games were about to begin. Athletes with disabilities from all over the world were ready to compete in 20 different events. Theoretical **physicist** and cosmologist Stephen Hawking was there to deliver the speech at the opening ceremony.

Stephen was surrounded by images of space as he gave his speech at the beginning of the opening ceremony.

"We are all different," Stephen said, speaking to the more than 4,300 athletes who surrounded the stage. "There is no such thing as the standard or run-of-the-mill human being. But we share the same human spirit. However difficult life may seem, there is always something you can do and succeed at."

And Stephen would know. For 55 years, he lived with a disease that robbed him of the ability to move and speak. But that did not stop him from becoming one of the world's most brilliant scientists. He was relentless in pursuing his goals and working to solve the mysteries of the universe.

In Theory

Theoretical physicists use experimental data and mathematical models. They propose unifying theories to explain **phenomena** in the universe. Sir Isaac Newton and Albert Einstein were other famous physicists. Cosmologists are physicists who study the universe on a very large scale. They often work to understand how the universe was formed, or how the size of the universe is changing over long periods of time. Neil deGrasse Tyson is also a cosmologist.

Paralympics—a series of international competitions for athletes with disabilities

phenomena—very unusual or remarkable events

Stephen William Hawking was born in Oxford, England, on January 8, 1942. His father, Frank, was a medical researcher specializing in tropical diseases. His mother, Isobel, was a secretary for a medical research institute. Stephen had two younger sisters, Philippa and Mary, and a brother, Edward Frank David.

Mary said young Stephen was "always into things." When their father built a dollhouse for her, Stephen installed plumbing and lighting.

Stephen was born exactly 300 years after the death of Galileo Galilei.

His cousin Sarah Hardenberg recalled Stephen had his eyes set far beyond Earth.

"He would spend a lot of time looking up at the sky, looking at the stars, and wondering where eternity came to an end," she said.

Stephen's parents taught him to question things and think big. His family discussed and debated all kinds of subjects and there were plenty of books in their home.

"It was a place where my mind was constantly challenged," he said.

Galileo

Galileo Galilei was an Italian physicist and **astronomer**. He studied the stars, planets, and other natural objects in space. Galileo was the first person to look at the moon through a telescope. He also confirmed the theory that Earth and all other planets revolve around the sun.

astronomer—a scientist who studies stars, planets, and other objects in space

During his school years, Stephen was not considered the most successful student.

"I was never more than about halfway up the class," Stephen said. "My classwork was very untidy, and my handwriting was the despair of my teachers."

Yet his classmates nicknamed him Einstein. In his teens, Stephen built model airplanes and boats. He invented complicated board games. In high school, he and his friends built a computer for solving logic problems. As Stephen considered college, he decided to pursue a degree in natural sciences specializing in **physics**.

At age 17 Stephen received a **scholarship** to Oxford University. There, he became interested in **cosmology**. However, he was bored with his studies.

cosmology—the science of the origin and development of the universe

physics—the study of matter and energy

scholarship—a grant or prize that pays for a student to go to college or to follow a course of study

The small city of Oxford is home to two large universities. More than 40,000 residents are college students.

"I once calculated that I did about a thousand hours' work in the three years I was there, an average of an hour a day," Stephen said.

College was easy. But Stephen's life was about to become more complicated. In his third and final year at Oxford, he became increasingly clumsy. One night, he tumbled down a flight of stairs. The fall was so hard that he lost consciousness and forgot where he was. He recovered and brushed it off.

"I didn't realize at the time it was a warning sign of things to come," Stephen said.

In 1962 Stephen passed the exam required to earn a degree in natural science. He graduated with first-class honors and received a scholarship to Cambridge University. He would pursue an advanced degree in cosmology. Cambridge is where he began his research on the stars and the origins of the universe.

Cambridge University celebrated its 800th anniversary in 2009.

At Christmas, Stephen fell while skating and could not get up. Shortly after his 21st birthday, he was diagnosed with amyotrophic lateral sclerosis, or ALS. The disease destroys the nerves that control the body's muscles. Doctors told Stephen he had two to three years to live. He returned to Cambridge but found it difficult to focus. Why continue when he wouldn't live long enough to finish his PhD?

ALS

ALS is a disease that weakens the muscles. Walking, talking, eating, and even breathing become difficult. It is usually diagnosed between the ages of 40 and 60. There is no known cure. Only about 5 percent of patients live more than 20 years after their diagnoses.

ALS is also called Lou Gehrig's disease, after the New York Yankees baseball player. He died at age 37 in 1941, two years after he was diagnosed with ALS.

3 BE DETERMINED

Stephen found the motivation he needed when he met Jane Wilde at a party. After they were engaged, Stephen threw himself into his work again. For the first time in his life, he put an effort into his studies. To his surprise, he was enjoying himself.

Stephen wanted to answer the major scientific question of the time: Did the universe have a beginning? Many scientists were opposed to the **big bang** theory. Physicist Roger Penrose was developing an idea about what happens to a star when it collapses under the force of its own **gravity**. He thought the star would crush itself to a tiny point of infinite **density**. In that point, time would stop. That point would be the center of a black hole. Penrose called that point a singularity.

The name "black hole" was coined in 1967 by physicist John Wheeler. The first black hole was discovered in 1971.

Black Holes

A black hole is a place in space with intense gravity. **Matter** is squeezed into a tiny space. Light cannot escape a black hole. Because of this, black holes are invisible. Only specially designed space telescopes can help find black holes.

big bang—theory that a sudden event caused the beginning of the universe
density—the amount of mass an object or substance has based on a unit of volume
gravity—a force that pulls objects with mass together
matter—particles of which everything in the universe is made

Stephen theorized that the universe began as a singularity. Before that, there was nothing. The universe spontaneously created itself in the big bang. His findings changed the way scientists thought about the beginning of the universe. They also earned him a paid research **fellowship** at Cambridge.

In March 1966 Stephen completed his PhD. The next year, his son Robert, was born. A daughter, Lucy, came in 1970.

Stephen's health worsened in 1969. He had started using a cane, then crutches, and finally a wheelchair. Despite his physical struggles, he made another major discovery. When two black holes collide and merge, the surface area of the new black hole grows bigger. It never decreases in size. This discovery became known as the second law of black hole dynamics.

fellowship—an academic research position at a university

Stephen and Jane were married on July 14, 1965. At this time, he needed a cane to walk. Stephen, Jane, Robert, and Lucy are pictured here in 1978.

An illustration of Hawking radiation shows particles escaping a black hole.

Stephen continued to work, even as his voice weakened and his speech became slurred. He found out what happens to **particles** at the edge of a black hole. Previously it was believed that nothing escaped a black hole. But in 1974 Stephen concluded that black holes must emit particles. Eventually the black holes could shrink, and then vanish. His discovery became known as Hawking **radiation**. A few weeks later, Stephen was inducted into the Royal Society, a scientific society that also included legends Sir Isaac Newton and Charles Darwin.

Climate Change

In 2017 Stephen made another prediction. He said the damage being done to Earth through **climate change** was destroying the planet. He described it as "one of the great dangers we face, and it's one we can prevent if we act now."

climate change—a significant change in Earth's climate over a period of time

particle—an extremely tiny piece of matter

radiation—tiny particles sent out from radioactive material

The California Institute of Technology invited Stephen to be a visiting professor in 1974. When he and his family arrived, he was still able to write equations. Because of ALS, he could no longer write by the end of the year. He began to visualize the universe in his mind instead.

The California Institute of Technology, or Caltech, is the setting of the TV show *The Big Bang Theory*. Stephen appeared as a guest star on the show multiple times.

California Institute of Technology

Stephen at Cambridge, 1975

Meanwhile, the awards kept coming. Pope Paul VI honored him with the Gold Medal for Science in 1975. In 1978 he was awarded the Albert Einstein Medal. In 1979 he became the Lucasian Professor of Mathematics at Cambridge. In the midst of it all, Stephen and Jane welcomed their third child, Timothy, in 1979.

DID YOU KNOW?

Since 1663 there have only been 19 Lucasian Professors of Mathematics. Others include Sir Isaac Newton and Charles Babbage.

After receiving the Order of the British Empire from Queen Elizabeth II in 1982, Stephen began writing a book on the origins of the universe. But while vacationing in Switzerland in 1985, he caught a chest infection. The infection developed into pneumonia. He could not breathe on his own and was placed on a life-support machine.

Doctors performed a tracheotomy. A tube was inserted into his windpipe. That connected him to a **ventilator**. It helped Stephen breathe, but he could no longer speak. To communicate, he had to spell words letter by letter. He would raise his eyebrow when someone pointed to the right letter on a spelling card.

DID YOU KNOW?

After his surgery, Stephen needed 24-hour-a-day medical care.

With the help of Equalizer, Stephen could communicate at a rate of 15 words per minute.

A computer expert in California named Walt Woltosz sent Stephen a computer program. The program, called Equalizer, allowed him to select words from menus on a screen by pressing a switch. The words were then converted into speech. This would become Stephen's **iconic** electronic voice.

iconic—widely viewed as perfectly capturing the meaning or spirit of something or someone

ventilator—a machine that helps people breathe

In 1988 Stephen published *A Brief History of Time: From the Big Bang to Black Holes*. It explained cosmology and the universe in a way that people who knew nothing about cosmology could understand. It remained on the best-seller list for many years.

Stephen wrote eight books. He also coauthored a number of books and collaborated on films and television shows.

With his book's success, Stephen began to travel the world. He was invited to give lectures, appear on talk shows, and make TV appearances. He was even invited to be on his favorite sci-fi show, *Star Trek*. In later years, he wrote other books, including *Black Holes and Baby Universes*, *The Universe in a Nutshell*, and *The Grand Design*. He and his daughter, Lucy, also wrote a series of science-based adventure books for children.

The stress of living in the public eye took its toll on Stephen and Jane's marriage and they divorced in 1995. They remained friends. Stephen married his former nurse, Elaine Mason, that same year. They divorced in 2006.

DID YOU KNOW?

A Brief History of Time has sold more than 10 million copies worldwide. It has been translated into more than 30 different languages. In 1998 it earned a *Guinness Book of World Records* title for being an all-time best-seller.

In 2007 Stephen was thrilled to experience weightlessness in a zero-gravity flight. He had wanted to be one of the first private citizens to travel into space. In 2016 billionaire Richard Branson offered Stephen a place on his space plane, *SpaceShipTwo*. Stephen is the only person ever offered a free seat.

Authorities had been worried about letting someone with ALS experience zero-gravity. The success of Stephen's flight allowed a group of children who used wheelchairs to take a zero-gravity flight too.

"The long-term survival of the human race is at risk as long as it is confined to a single planet," he has said. "Sooner or later, disasters such as an asteroid collision or nuclear war could wipe us all out. But once we spread out into space and establish independent colonies, our future should be safe."

Stephen was awarded the United States's highest civilian honor, the Presidential Medal of Freedom, in 2009. By that time, Stephen could no longer operate his wheelchair the regular way. His eyeglasses controlled his speech synthesizer. The glasses had a sensor that responded to his cheek movement. But he kept working.

Music and the Multiverse

In 2015 Zayn Malik left the boy band One Direction. Stephen was asked about the event's cosmological effect. Stephen took the question seriously. "One day there may well be proof of multiple universes," he said. "And in that universe Zayn is still in One Direction."

Stephen was an advocate for people with disabilities. He opposed budget cuts that would limit access to medical care. He pointed out how technology had enhanced his life.

In a video message to the United Nations Educational, Scientific and Cultural Organization (UNESCO), Stephen said, "We need to make sure this technology becomes available to those who need it so that no one lives in silence. Please listen to me. I speak for the people you can't hear."

In 2014 Stephen met the Queen of England at a charity event. She asked if he still spoke with an American accent. He replied that his voice was copyrighted.

Stephen also looked for ways to enhance the way he communicated. In 2011 he participated in a trial for a device called iBrain. It was designed to pick up changes in the wearer's electrical brain signals. A person's thoughts were translated into spikes on a grid.

"I wish to assist in research, encourage investment in this area, and, most importantly, to offer some future hope to people diagnosed with ALS and other **neurodegenerative** conditions," he said.

Giving Back

Stephen was a big supporter of the Motor Neurone Disease Association. Its campaign "Don't let me die without a voice" spoke to him. When Stephen died, the association's website crashed because so many people wanted to leave a donation in Stephen's name. His wheelchair was auctioned off, with part of the proceeds going to the association.

neurodegenerative—the breakdown of the body's nervous system, especially the brain

Stephen spent his final days busy on his last work, *A Smooth Exit from Eternal Inflation*. He predicted that the universe will end when stars run out of energy. He also theorized that scientists could find alternate universes using **probes**. The paper was finished 10 days before his death.

Stephen died on March 14, 2018, in Cambridge, at age 76. His ashes were buried between the graves of Charles Darwin and Sir Isaac Newton at Westminster Abbey in London, England. Etched on his gravestone was his equation for Hawking radiation. As his ashes were lowered into the ground, a message was sent into space. Stephen's words of peace and hope were beamed toward the nearest known black hole in the universe, still thousands of light-years away.

probe—a small spacecraft sent to gather data

Stephen lived each day fearlessly and to the fullest. He demonstrated the power of the human mind and spirit. He spoke for science and for those with disabilities. He also inspired many to further explore the cosmos and build a better future for everyone.

"Try to make sense of what you see and about what makes the universe exist. Be curious," Stephen said. "We are all time travelers, journeying together into the future. But let us work together to make that future a place we want to visit."

GLOSSARY

astronomer (uh-STRAH-nuh-muhr)—a scientist who studies stars, planets, and other objects in space

big bang—theory that a sudden event caused the beginning of the universe

climate change (KLY-muht CHAYNJ)—a significant change in Earth's climate over a period of time

cosmology (kahz-MAH-luh-jee)—the science of the origin and development of the universe

density (DEN-si-tee)—the amount of mass an object or substance has based on a unit of volume

fellowship (FELL-oh-ship)—an academic research position at a university

gravity (GRAV-uh-tee)—a force that pulls objects with mass together

iconic (EYE-cahn-ik)—widely viewed as perfectly capturing the meaning or spirit of something or someone

matter (MAT-ur)—particles of which everything in the universe is made

neurodegenerative (NUR-oh-DUH-gen-uhr-uh-tiv)—the breakdown of the body's nervous system, especially the brain

Paralympics (pa-ruh-LIM-piks)—a series of international competitions for athletes with disabilities

particle (PAR-tuh-kuhl)—an extremely tiny piece of matter; particles are too small to be seen with the naked eye

phenomena (fe-NOM-uh-nuh)—very unusual or remarkable events

physics (FIZ-iks)—the study of matter and energy, including light, heat, electricity, and motion

probe (PROHB)—a small spacecraft sent to gather data

radiation (ray-dee-AY-shuhn)—tiny particles sent out from radioactive material

scholarship (SKOL-ur-ship)—a grant or prize that pays for a student to go to college or to follow a course of study

ventilator (VEN-tuh-lay-tuhr)—a machine that helps people breathe

READ MORE

Gigliotti, Jim E. *Who Was Stephen Hawking?* New York: Penguin Workshop, 2019.

Hawking, Stephen. *Brief Answers to the Big Questions.* New York: Bantam Books, an imprint of Random House, 2018.

Wood, Alix. *Stephen Hawking.* New York: PowerKids Press, 2019.

INTERNET SITES

Black Holes: Facts, Theory, and Definition
https://www.space.com/15421-black-holes-facts-formation-discovery-sdcmp.html

NASA—Black Hole Explorer
https://www.nasa.gov/audience/foreducators/5-8/features/F_Black_Hole_Explorer.html

Stephen Hawking
http://www.hawking.org.uk/

CRITICAL THINKING QUESTIONS

1. Stephen was only 21 years old when he was diagnosed with ALS. Doctors told him he had only a few years left to live. If you were given this news, how would you feel? What would you do with the time you had left?

2. Physicists work to understand and explain the world around us. Sometimes they are things we can see but are not easy to explain. Pretend you are Sir Isaac Newton. How would you explain gravity to another person?

3. Stephen lived with ALS for 55 years. This is much longer than the average patient. What factors do you think helped extend his life?

INDEX